John Bates: Britich Fashion Designer

The Sensational Years, 1963-1968

Frederic A. Sharf *with* Michelle Finamore

ACKNOWLEDGEMENTS

Transparencies.
See through
White organza
scattered in
daisy motifs
over
small shorts.
JEAN VARON.
'67

This publication was printed and bound by Velocity Print Solutions, Middlebury, CT.

ISBN-10: 0-9839573-6-3
ISBN-13: 978-0-9839573-6-2

Library of Congress Control Number:
A catalog record for this book is available from the Library of Congress.

FIRST EDITION

Printed in the United States of America

Many people have helped me to assemble this book.

A special thanks to **John Siggins** for numerous helpful responses to my questions, and to John Bates for his cooperation. **Leslie Verrinder** traveled several times to Wales to meet with Mr. Bates and Mr. Siggins. Leslie then packed the Archive for shipment to my office. **Pam Parmal**, **Lauren Whitley**, **Michelle Finamore** from the Fashion Department at Museum of Fine Arts, Boston have been terrific colleagues. The John Bates Archive now resides permanently at that famous art museum. I am pleased that **Chris Collins** of Brigham and Women's Hospital enthusiastically endorsed placement of the exhibition in the Sharf Admitting Center. The exhibit was installed by **Mark Wallison**. Patients have already commented in positive terms.

Michelle Finamore has provided helpful text. **Paul Cyr** has designed this beautiful book. Photographs of the art were taken by Paul and Mark Wallison. **Margie Phillips**, my office associate, has provided invaluable electronic support.

In 2006, the Fashion Museum, Bath, England organized an exhibition of John Bates vintage clothing; in 2008 the Antique Collectors Club, Woodbridge, England published a biographical study of John's career, written by Richard Lester with foreword by Marit Allen. I am honored to follow in their footsteps.

Frederic A. Sharf
April 15, 2013

CONTENTS

left: **Design for Pants Outfit with High Stand-up Ruffled Collar**
Date: 1967 for Cilla Black

opposite: **Design for Mini-Dress with Hipster Shorts and Bra Top.**
Date: 1966/1967 for Jean Veron

PREFACE

Design for Mini-Dress with Full-Length Sleeves
and Ruffle Scarf

Date: 1967

Opposite: **Design for Peasant-Look Evening Dress**

Date: 1967/1968 for Jean Varon

This exotic look became popular at the end of
the decade.

In April 2012 I agreed to purchase the Archive of John
Bates in order to donate this Archive to the Museum
of Fine Arts, Boston.

Over the past ten years I have worked with Pam
Parmal, Director of the Textile and Fashion
Department at the Museum, to build a collection of
20th Century fashion art (design drawings as well as
advertising artwork) and supporting documentary
material (scrapbooks, photo albums, letters).

We felt that John Bates was a perfect fit with other
material which the Museum owns; and we felt that
his art could be exhibited in various contexts.

Quite by accident the Brigham and Women's
Hospital, a world famous Boston institution, asked
me to develop an exhibition which would focus on
the 1960s. For ten years I have installed art exhibitions
in the Sharf Admitting Center, where all patients are
admitted. In many instances these exhibitions then
go on to art museums under the auspices of MFA,
Boston.

These exhibitions provide an opportunity to explore
various artists; and to conduct research; and to
produce publications. John Bates is a wonderful
addition to this heritage.

A word of thanks to my colleague Michelle Finamore,
a well known fashion scholar, and curator at MFA,
Boston. She has added a professional perspective to
this book, and to my project.

Frederic A. Sharf
April 2013

John Bates: British Fashion Designer

The Sensational Years, 1963-1968 | Frederic A. Sharf

John Bates with a Model, circa 1965

opposite: **Design for Mini-Dress with Op-Art Fabric**
Date: 1966/1967
Sleeves and skirt with scalloped edge, and
Op-Art fabric.

I

John Bates was born in 1935 in the small Northumberland village of Dinnington, seven miles from Newcastle. His father was a coal miner. John wanted to be a journalist. After attending primary school in Dinnington, and then secondary school in Newcastle, he went to a secretarial college in Newcastle to learn typing and shorthand.

In 1953 he was conscripted into the British Army. He went through basic training at Aldershot, and then was assigned to clerical duty at the War Office in central London. He resided in a rented room just off Trafalgar Square.

His service at the War Office coincided with the Mau Mau uprising in Kenya which often meant late evenings dealing with dispatches from the battleground. John loved living in London; he knew he would not return to Newcastle.

He was a talented sketch artist. Mutual friends arranged entry level employment with the London couturier Herbert Sidon. Sidon's price points were a notch below Norman Hartnell and Hardy Amies. His clients ranged from cafe society to working women. John remained there from 1955 until 1957.

His assignments at Sidon's premises on Sloane Street were menial. He would later jokingly characterize his job as picking up pins. However, Sidon encouraged John to sketch clothing designs in his spare time; occasionally these sketches were translated into actual garments. After learning the fashion business in Sidon's salon, John decided to resign in 1957. He wanted to concentrate on developing and selling his own designs to dress shops.

II

Selling design drawings was not an easy way to make a living. In 1959 John accepted an offer from Diana Dresses on Edgeware Road to join their staff as a designer and pattern cutter. This firm manufactured low priced ladies clothing. Their customers were chain stores. This seemed like a useful experience, and a way to learn the manufacturing business. He lived within walking distance on Portobello Road.

A chance encounter in 1959 reconnected John with two Irish businessmen who he had met while working for Herbert Sidon. Eric West and Bernard Bragg wanted to invest in the fashion business and proposed backing John. They had always remembered the sketches he had showed them two years earlier at Sidon's.

The new firm was established in the fall of 1959 under the name Jean Varon. They hoped that the French sound would attract attention. They operated from a first floor flat in Ladbrooke Grove. The business flourished by making wearable clothes which responded to then current market demands.

In 1961 the partners decided that the business would grow faster if they were located in the fashion district. They moved to a first floor space at No.17 Woodstock Street, off of Bond Street. The office and showroom were on the first floor; manufacturing and storage was on an upper floor.

Fenwick of Bond Street approached John in the spring of 1961 to see if he could create wedding dresses. This was certainly a new challenge. In June 1961 the Sunday Times featured a wedding dress from this collection; it was the first appearance in print of the Jean Varon label. His designs were beautiful and affordable. The Jean Varon label was now a factor in the London fashion world.

John Bates in his studio, circa 1967

III

Wallis Shops on Oxford Street at Marble Arch was an important retail presence in 1960s London. In 1962 Harold Wallis came to the Woodstock Street showroom to review the Jean Varon line. He placed large orders for day dresses and short evening dresses. All dresses were to be cut above the knee.

The Wallis orders were so large that production could not be accomplished at Woodstock Street. For the first time outside sources were retained. These workers were personally selected by John Bates and his partner Eric West. Production of the garments of the outsourced vendors was reviewed regularly to assure that quality standards were maintained.

The Jean Varon label was well established in 1962 and 1963. Many new shops placed orders. The business was expanding. The press was taking notice. *Women's Mirror Magazine* in August 1963 featured Julie Christie on the cover wearing a Jean Varon dress. The line was featured in the September 1963 issue of *Vanity Fair*; and in the November 1963 issue of *Flair Magazine*.

IV

By the final months of 1963 the Jean Varon line was well known for beautifully styled ready-to-wear, both daywear and evening wear. The designs were feminine, and flattered a woman's body. Young women in London were wearing short skirts; Paris designers like Cardin and Courreges endorsed this new look.

A few buyers for American department stores began in 1963 to sample the Jean Varon line. But the breakout year for the so-called London Look was 1964. The British invasion of American consumers really

Organza + lace see through to figure.

JOHN BATES.

Design for Mini-Dress with See-Through Midriff.

Date: 1966/1967 for Jean Veron

Note instructions to workroom.

started with the February 9, 1964 appearance of the Beatles on the Ed Sullivan TV show. The youthful exuberance which characterized many new London fashion labels was popularized in the United States by the music of the Beatles and the Rolling Stones.

In the spring of 1964 John Bates was invited to join a British trade mission to the United States. The group arrived in New York City on May 28th. It was the first of many trips to the United States for John. The group was composed of young designers. Their exhibition in New York successfully launched their designs in the United States.

Now the American press began to follow these designers. On June 3, 1964 the well known *New York Times* fashion critic Bernardine Morris wrote: "British designers are producing a new breed of fashion ... young, exuberant, and occasionally zany ..." London became recognized as the new worldwide fashion center for its creativity and innovation. On September 29, 1964 the *New York Times* reported that the young London fashion designers "had seized the fashion limelight" and their clothing was "fresh, amusing, a new clothes image that is the property of the young."

On September 18, 1964 *Womens Wear Daily* wrote that John was "rebellious, effervescent, dedicated." He was the "cornerstone of London's new school ... his work runs from the fairly zany to the classic." John was selling wearable feminine clothing to well known American retailers such as Bendels, Bloomingdale's, Macy's and Gimbels.

He introduced an entirely new fashion idea in the United States in the summer of 1964 when fashion magazines ran photos of models wearing his short skirts with long stockings in matching fabric.

When American buyers visited London Fashion Week in October 1964 they were blown away by the new styles. One buyer reported to The *New York Times* that there was "more excitement and individuality of design" in London than could be found in the United States. When Diana Vreeland presented British fashion in the January 1965 issue of *Vogue* under the title "Youthquake 1965" she officially launched the London Look in the United States.

The January 1965 issue of British Vogue featured a John Bates dress which he called "Kasbah" modeled by Jean Shrimpton, the very best of the young British fashion models. The skirt was short; the midriff was made with see-thru fabric. This presentation established the 1965 fashion direction.

Jean Varon had grown large enough to warrant a professional management team within the company and an outside public relations organization. The Jean Varon PR account was handled by John Siggins. John had spent eight years working in Africa for the British American Tobacco Company prior to his return to London. His presence was so valuable to John Bates that Siggins was brought inside the company in 1966.

With a strong organization behind him John Bates could devote all his energy in 1965 to producing new designs. A photo of a model wearing a Jean Varon short skirt appeared in the press with a caption "short-short, the length the British girls insist on..." On March 28, 1965 The *New York Times* wrote that young British designers "are churning out quantities of original, bright and inexpensive clothes."

In June 1965 John was quite suddenly contacted by the producers of a very successful TV show called The Avengers. They wanted to give their lead character Emma Peel a new look. The series would begin again in October 1965 with a new actress Diana Rigg as Mrs. Peel. John was given a few days to produce designs.

Dress design for Diana Rigg "The Avengers"

Date: 1965

White crepe embroidered in navy and red braid and studded in navy and red to match. White shoes with cut out sides and shadow stripe legs.

There was no time for formal introductions. John was given a script, and a description of the heroine's lifestyle. He began to sketch. Within four days he was ready with his first design. The sketch went to his workroom where a rough garment was constructed. John reviewed the result, and once satisfied his cutter made a garment ready for fitting.

John was hired to design clothing, shoes, and accessories for Diana Rigg. The show was already in production but the look for the new season was not revealed. On July 11, 1965 The *Sunday London Times* ran the initial press release under the title "Mystery A La Mod", with a photo of John and Diana looking at the secret design drawings.

John's designs were entirely black and white. Elements of Op-Art were incorporated which reflected John's fascination with the work of the British artist Bridgit Riley. The producers wanted to take John's designs for Diana Rigg and create a small, saleable collection which could be brought to market quickly by licensing some well known British ready-to-wear manufacturers. The collection would be marketed as The Jean Varon Avengers Collection designed by John Bates.

In August 1965 the group of licensed manufacturers met for the first time at a special "trade only" fashion show where they were introduced to the entire collection. When the TV show began to air in October the response was CRAZY.

At London Fashion Week, October 1965 the London Fashion House Group exhibited at the Hilton on Park Lane the Jean Varon mini-skirt dresses in op-art designs with matching ribbed stockings which had been popularized by the initial airings of the Avengers. This group traveled at the end of October to New York on the QE2 for an exhibition entitled British Fashions-USA'66 which opened on board the liner. When the models went ashore wearing the new mini-skirts they were mobbed. The *New York Times* announced on November 5th "The British Have Arrived." Buyers went to the Plaza Hotel to place orders.

VII

The fall of 1965 was notable in the fashion world for the opening of a new boutique called Paraphernalia. The shop was located on Madison Avenue between 66th and 67th streets, and only carried women's clothing by young designers (including John Bates). The genius behind this venture was Paul Young.

Paul had been a buyer for J. C. Penney. He had visited London in 1963 and 1964 as their buyer, and had fallen in love with the new swinging London look. He attempted to convince Penney management to back him in a shop which would sell this new fashion. When Penney would not back him he resigned and turned to a well known 7th Avenue RTW manufacturer, Puritan, for backing.

John Bates recalled meeting Young in London, either late in 1964 or early in 1965. He was introduced by Marit Allen, an editor at British *Vogue*. John also met Sandy Moss, a former fashion model, who was working for Paul as his buyer in London for the new shop.

Once the shop opened in October 1965 its success was instantaneous. Within a few years they had more than 20 stores allover the United States. This shop was the flagship for the London Look, and John Bates was one important part of this look. His business in the United States expanded to every state except Alaska. The success of Paraphernalia and the success of the Jean Varon line in America in the years from 1965 to the end of the decade were two important aspects of the expansion of the London Look.

VIII

In order to fully understand the excitement which John Bates had generated by 1966 it is useful to look at a few aspects of his schedule that year. On June 15th he attended a press luncheon at the London Hilton where the finalists were announced for the prestigious Yardley London Look Award. John was one of the finalists and presented a small selection of his work. The various presentations were filmed for later use.

In July his friend Lady Clare Rendlesham, former fashion editor of *Queen Magazine*, asked John to submit a few designs for Audrey Hepburn to consider using in a movie entitled *Two for the Road* with Albert Finney. The movie had already started shooting. John decided to send some variations on one theme,—a cape. Audrey's reply arrived in September. She liked all of them, so the final selection would be up to John. However, he was traveling and far too busy to follow up this project. He never did meet Audrey.

In August Jean Varon was invited to present a fashion show at the annual International Red Cross Ball held in the Casino at Juan Les Pins on the Riviera. The previous year Yves St. Laurent had presented his collection to the assembled wealthy attendees. The headline Act for 1966 was Dick Haymes, a popular singer whose career was on the decline.

Poncho design for Audrey Hepburn
Date: 1966
Sleeves and skirt with fringe.

Lace poncho

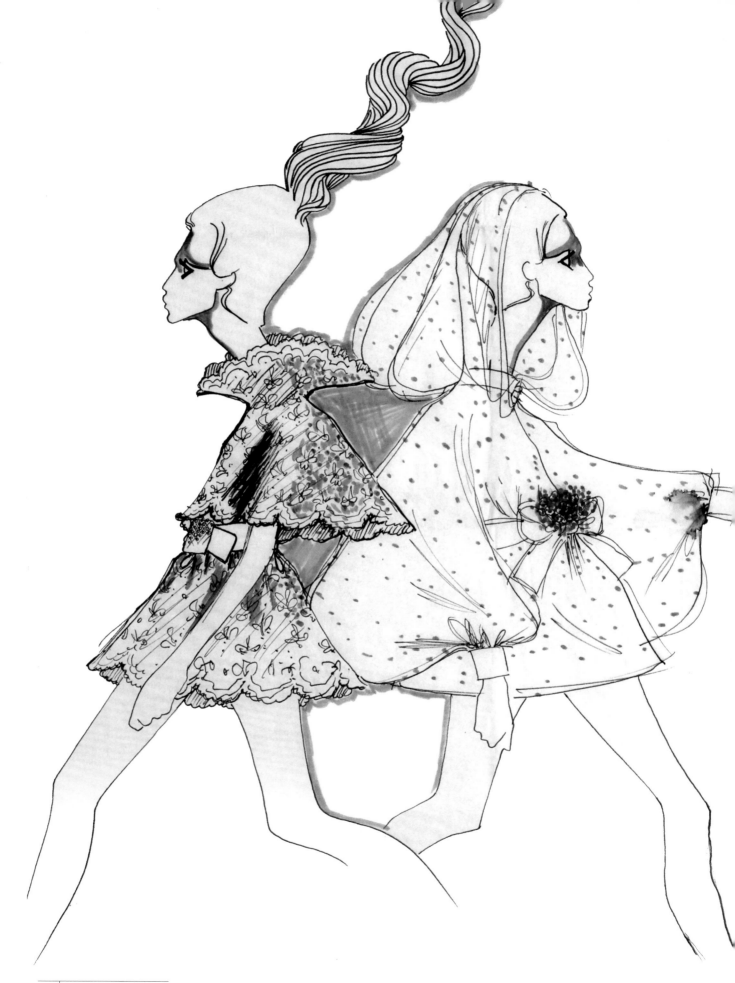

The Jean Varon group of 11 people arrived at Nice Airport. Six models were wearing the latest London Look short skirts. The group was transported to the Casino on a fire engine, creating quite a scene en route. John Bates had planned to have his fashion show accompanied by Beatles music but the Casino orchestra had never heard of the Beatles.

Across the street John spotted the famous nightclub Whiskey a Go Go. Their band knew the Beatles music. He borrowed them for his Casino show, and in return did a repeat show the next night at their club. Both events were sensational. Jean Varon received numerous orders for their mod clothing.

Early in September John traveled to New York City where he was announced winner of the Yardley London Look Award for 1966. On the 14th of September he made a personal appearance at Gimbels to promote Jean Varon. He was a big star!

At the end of September he was back in London to attend the filming preview of the movie which had been made in June of the Yardley Fashion Show. On November 8th he was back in New York City for a two week fashion presentation at the Plaza Hotel.

Meanwhile, the explosion in sales meant that larger premises were needed. In the fall of 1966 Jean Varon entered into a long term lease at 19-20 Noel Street. Offices, showrooms, and workrooms were now housed in 6,500 square feet. Susan Jarrett handled the showroom; John Siggins handled press liason and all public relations.

The pace of life was now so hectic that it would ultimately be one factor in the decision by John Bates to close the business.

bove: **Op-Art Designs for Mini-Dress**

)ate: 1965

ght: **John Bates receiving Yardley London ook Award, 1966**

pposite: **Poncho Design Variations for udrey Hepburn**

)ate: 1966

eturned to John Bates by Miss Hepburn ith note saying she liked all designs, and e must make the final choice.

The London ready-to-wear industry has a distinctive rhythm. Collections must be prepared for two major seasons. The Spring and Summer collections need to be launched the previous September. The Autumn and Winter collections are launched the previous April. In addition a winter mid-season collection would be launched the previous November; and a mid-season summer collection the previous February.

To properly prepare for these seasons, designers needed to look at fabrics two or three times in any years. The fabric shows meant travel to France or Italy. John Bates drew inspiration from the fabrics he selected. John Siggins was a helpful advisor in building a balanced collection. Siggins knew that a few sexy pieces would attract the media. Stylish, wearable pieces were the bread-and-butter.

John Bates sketched each collection. Hundreds of sketches were required to obtain exactly the right look. Each collection needed to be aimed at their typical customer: a young woman who needed inexpensive, yet stylish daywear and evening wear. These women ranged from debutantes to secretaries; and to the fast growing group of young women working in the business world.

X

The big news for 1967 was Cilla Black, the biggest selling British recording artist of the 1960s. Born Priscilla Maria Veronica White on 27 May 1963 in the toughest part of Liverpool she made her name singing in the local clubs where she was known as "Swinging Cilla". When a local Liverpool newspaper mistakenly featured her as Cilla Black she decided to keep that name.

In 1963 she was signed by Brian Epstein, the Beatles manager. He wanted to add a female vocalist to their small organization. She began to sing songs written for her by John Lennon and Paul McCartney. She recorded at their Abbey Road Studio in London.

In the summer of 1967 she was signed to star in a BBC-TV show simply called "Cilla". She was brought to the Jean Varon showroom by Peter Brown, road manager of the Beatles. Brown was a friend of Eric West, the business partner of John Bates.

During the summer and fall of 1967 Cilla and John, collaborated on outfits to be worn on the TV show. John had a great sense of what would work; and Cilla trusted his judgment. The first show aired on January 30th, 1968. John continued to design for two more seasons of the TV show, as well as for her stage and cabaret appearances. He even designed her wedding dress worn in, January 1969. However, he did no attend the wedding.

Design for Suede Mini-Dress with Fringes
Date: 1967 for Cilla Black

POSTSCRIPT

While our study of John Bates deliberately focused on the 1960s, a brief word is in order to complete his story in the fashion world.

The Jean Varon label was successful throughout the 1970s. In the fall of 1974 a John Bates label was launched. This new label was identified as luxury ready-to-wear, or "almost couture."

Designing two separate collections increased the hectic lifestyle for John Bates and John Siggins. They had become life partners in 1966.

The last designs were for Spring 1980. The collections were well received. However, they had decided to close the company. The John Bates label was simply closed; the Jean Varon label was sold. The *Times* of London reported on October 14,1 980 that the process of going out of business was completed.

During the 1980s the continued to reside in London and engage in some wholesale and mail order work. In 1990 they moved to Wales. In 1995 they abandoned all commercial activity. They quite liked the rural lifestyle of their seaside house. John Siggins likes to garden; John Bates likes to paint.

Design for Fake Fur Jacket

Date: 1969/1970

Drawn for *The Observer* Newspaper.
Worn by Twiggy, the most well known
model of 1960s/1970s.

John Bates on runway with model, circa1975

John Bates adjusting the outfit of his model in
preparation for a runway appearance, circa1968

John Bates: Original Drawings for **Jean Varon**

John Bates did business in the 1960s under his trade name Jean Varon. He selected this name for its French association; in addition there was nobody in the London telephone directory with the last name Varon. We have selected a few design drawings from the 1960s for his Jean Varon ready-to-wear line.

Design for Evening Dress with Empire Waist

Date: 1964/1965

Full length evening dresses were popular with teenagers in 1965. Often referred to as a granny-dress.

Three Op-Art Designs for Mini-Dress

Date: 1965

In 1965 John Bates was very interested in Op-Art paintings of the British artist Bridget Riley. He interpreted this popular art form in many dress designs.

opposite: **Three Designs for Mini-Dress**

Date: 1966/67

JOHN BATES.

BLACK AND WHITE MOSS CREPE.

Design for Mini-Dress with See-Through Midriff.

Date: 1966/1967

Note high ruffled collar with bow.

sign for Mini-Dress with Sleeves.
ate: 1966/1967
eves and skirt with fringe.

Transparencies.
See itrough
White organza
scattered in
daisy motifs
over
small shorts.
JEAN VARON.
'67

Design for Mini-Dress with Hipster Shorts and Bra Top.
Date: 1966/1967

Design for Mini-Dress with Tassels.

Date: 1966/1967
One piece dress with tassels at midriff.

Two Designs for Knee Length Dress with See-Through Accents

Date: 1966/1967

John Bates needed to include conventional dresses in his Jean Varon line.

brown, blue, purple studs
or white studs.

where "pink" —
is one layer of
organza, so
you can see
thro' on to flesh

JOHN
BATES.

Pink Tricel
insets
in organza
+
studded

Two Designs for Evening Dress

Date: 1966/1967

One design is knee-length; the other is full-length. Both have sleeves. Both are A-line, with accent at Empire waist.

Design for Evening Dress

Date: 1966/1967

A-line skirt, with bow accent at waist. Sleeveless with ruffled collar.

Cavendish Checks.

JOAN BATES
JEAN VARON.

Man's Full-Length Outer Coat, Military Style

Date: 1967/1968

Baccarat was a high style wholesaler, based in London. The owner was an old friend of John Bates.

MAXI LENGTH BROWN PURE NEW WOOL, LINED IN CREAM KALGAN LAMB.
OLD BRASS MILITARY BUTTONS AND BUCKLES.

JOHN BATES FOR BACCARAT

jean
VARON

Easy-to-wear mini-dress with blouse

Date: 1968

Opposite: **Space-Age Design for Outer Coat with Helmet Headwear**

Date: 1968/1969

All designers began to introduce space-age items into their collections at the end of the decade.

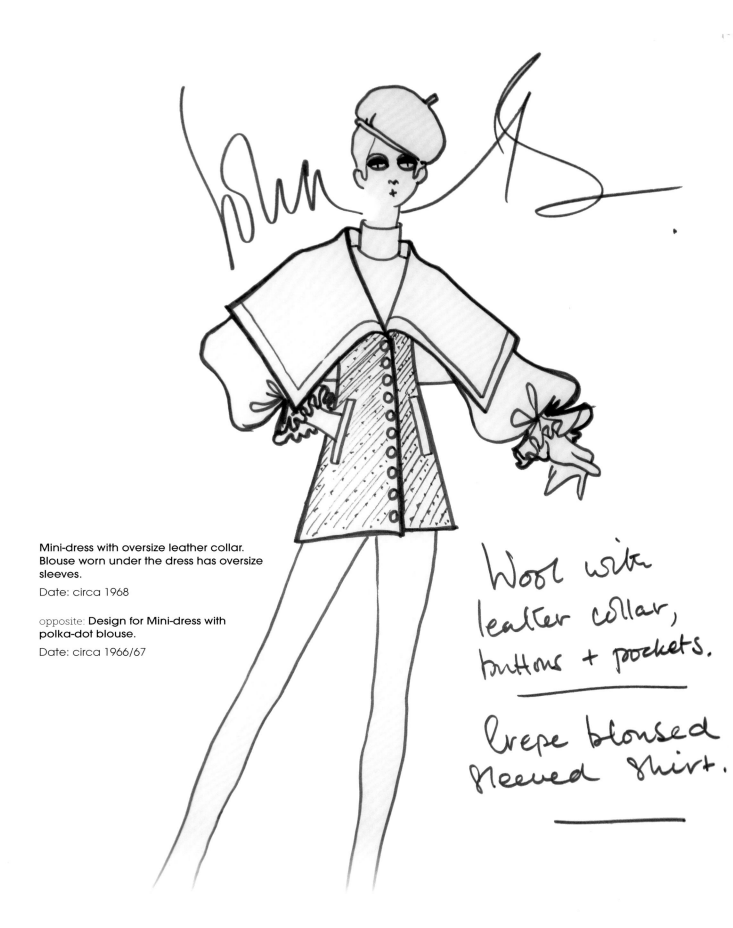

Mini-dress with oversize leather collar.
Blouse worn under the dress has oversize
sleeves.

Date: circa 1968

opposite: **Design for Mini-dress with
polka-dot blouse.**

Date: circa 1966/67

Wool with
leather collar,
buttons + pockets.

Crepe bloused
sleeved shirt.

**Mini-dress with Empire Waist
and Ruffled Sleeves**

Date: 1967

John Bates: Original Drawings for **Cilla Black**

The success which John Bates earned from his popular designs for The Avengers attracted the attention of the management team behind the Beatles. Their only female client was Cilla Black. In 1967 she was signed to do a TV show simply entitled Cilla. John Bates was selected to design her stage outfits. They were all unique, and never reproduced as ready-to-wear. A few of these designs follows.

Design for Mini-dress Outfit
Date: 1967

For Cilla Black.

Organza ins[ert]
Dotted with
beads.

JOHN BATES.

Design for Mini-Dress with Organza Insert
Date: 1967

Design for One-Piece Mini-Dress with Full Length Sleeves
Date: 1967

Design for Mini-Dress with Flared Sleeves

Date: 1967

Design for Mini-Dress with Flared Sleeves, which open as a See-Through Fan

Date: 1967

Two Mini-Dress Designs

Date: 1967

see through
Organza
inserts
lightly sprinkled
with embroidery.

JOHN BATES.
'67

Cilla Black.

Two Designs for Pants Outfit

Date: 1967

Very soft golden lamé.

Cilla Black.

Design for Pants Outfit with Crucifix Necklace

Date: 1967

Deisgn for Pants Outfit with Stand-up Collar
and Chain Belt

Date: 1967

Design for Skirt and Blouse Outfit
Date:1967

CB.

Organza top.
Stiff silky skirt

Diamonte
buckle + buttons.

C B. SHON

Design for Skirt, Blouse, Vest Outfit
Date:1967

The JEAN VARON

AVENGERS COLLECTION

designed by

JOHN BATES

THE AVENGERS

by John Bates

In 1965 I was approached by Anne Trehearne of *Queen Magazine* to see if I'd be interested in designing the wardrobe for a new actress called Diana Rigg in the new Avengers series.

I couldn't use anything from my own collection as they wanted to licence it out as the Avengers Collection, making it available to a huge young market throughout the U.K. after each weekly episode. The wardrobe consisted of coats, jackets, trousers, leathers, jumpsuits, dresses, furs, berets, a watch, tights, shoes, boots, gloves, shirts, and skirts—in fact, the lot! Everything had to be interchangeable and re-used within the series, so I used basic black and white, or pale colours that would photograph "white".

My first shock came with the first completed suit as filming was being held up—I delivered it, thankfully, on time, but was rung up the next day asking for Diana's first suit, as the one I'd delivered had gone straight on to the stuntman for the fight sequences and had been ripped to shreds!

For films and T.V. you need to be on your toes all of the day and sometimes evening to cope with ever changing schedules in indoor/ outdoor commitments, altered fight sequences, or re-takes. Something always happens to really test your abilities.

All the very hard work paid off handsomely. The series got rave reviews from everyone. The following day, every national newspaper gave whole pages to the clothes, as did *Vogue*, The *Sunday Times Magazine*, *The Observer*, *Queen*, and indeed all the glossy magazines, which helped enormously to make me, as they say, an overnight success.

I enjoyed very much working on the Avengers, but due to the need to concentrate on my own collections, I couldn't fit in another series. But it makes me laugh that after all this time, little bra tops, bare midriffs and short skirts are the norm for most pop groups, new fashion designers and fashion pundits!

The Jean Varon Avengers Collection
Catalog Cover
Date: 1965

JOHN
BATES

Diana Rigg
"The Avengers"

Black Stretch
Jersey and
Black stretch
ciré fight
suits.

"A Hurricane called Emma Dresses to Kill:"
Designs for **THE AVENGERS**

Michelle Finamore

In her first appearance as Emma Peel in *The Avengers*, Diana Rigg wears the ensemble most viewers already associated with the television series – a black catsuit. Mrs. Peel, as her partner John Steed addresses her, often dons the catsuit when she is ready for action. In the opening scene of "The Town of No Return," she is practicing her fencing moves and coyly convinces Steed to join her. The black knit catsuit, with a suggestive V-shaped leather bodice, allows her to move gracefully and speedily around her sleek, modern apartment. Throughout the show, and the series, she and Steed narrowly escape death time and again, yet viewers know that she will always overcome any threat, enabled by her confidence, poise, and her mod clothing. Her graphic ensembles by John Bates meld seamlessly with her screen persona, reflecting her spirited character and her physical prowess.

The strong modern heroine, participating in physical feats normally reserved for men, was not a new concept in the 1960s. There are popular culture precedents as early as the 1910s in serial dramas such as *The Perils of Pauline* and *The Adventures of Kathlyn*. *The Perils of Pauline* was a highly popular cliffhanger-style serial film that featured actress Pearl White barely escaping continued attempts on her life. Like Emma Peel, she eluded death with great panache and physical dexterity. Within the context of women fighting for the right to vote and other freedoms, such serial dramas were a natural development. During World War II, when women moved into what had been male-dominated professions, strong cinematic heroines emerged yet again. The increased accessibility of television in the early 1960s coincided with yet another wave of feminism, and the sexual revolution, and both movements posed a challenge to traditional gender roles. Such cultural shifts are embodied in the figure of Emma Peel and in the clothing that John Bates designed for *The Avengers*.

◆

In 1965 John Bates was hired by the Associated British Corporation to dress the fourth season of the highly successful spy-fi series. At the behest of Annie Trehearne, the former fashion editor of Queen magazine, the television company hired Bates to take the place of Jean Muir, who had unexpectedly stepped down from the job. Threhearne was familiar with Bates's work and insightfully perceived that his design sensibility would be a good fit for the show. Bates had less than a week to design clothing for the show and for an actress he had never met, yet Trehearne's instincts were right. Bates' fashion designs were perfectly attuned to the modern, youthful, and vibrant character of Emma Peel.

◆

Diana Rigg's predecessor actress Honor Blackman was the first in the role to wear a leather catsuit, which was an immediate sensation and became inextricably linked to the show and to the character. Designer Michael Whittaker, who had been brought onto the show by Blackman, created the leather ensembles, in a process which Blackman described as "pure accident." Leather was chosen for practical reasons; they needed a material strong enough to withstand the character's aggressive physicality. Bates retained the catsuit, but modernized it; instead of an outfit that was often described as "kinky" by the press, he succeeded in bringing it more in line with contemporary fashion trends.

opposite: **Two Designs for Fighting suit**

Date: 1965

Fighting Suit or Catsuit was John Bates interpretation of traditional jumpsuit. Designed for Diana Rigg to wear in TV series The Avengers.

Bates also expanded Mrs. Peels' wardrobe to include a much broader range of materials and styles that appealed to both the "feminine" and "masculine" side of her character. This dual aspect of her personality is established in the opening titles to the series. It begins with Emma moving about lithely in her leather catsuit, frozen in various stylized karate moves. Yet tellingly it closes with Emma in a soft ruffled blouse, wearing a formal up-do, and delicately sniffing a flower. It was important to communicate the right mix of sexy and sweet in both her character and the clothing designs, as well as playing up the "M appeal" or "man appeal" which was the source of her name.

Bates created fashions for an Emma empowered by both her masculine and feminine sides, exemplified in the catsuit in figure 1. The suit is made of black leather, buckled to one side, and has a deep V that exposes a roll neck ivory crepe blouse with full sleeves. The mixing of the "hard" leather with the "soft" crepe is an inventive way of dealing with her dual personality. Bates also created a similar design in figure 2 that is a catsuit entirely made of crepe—yet another a cunning inversion of the form, with the crepe moderating the somewhat masculine look of the outfit. Some journalists criticized Bates's ensembles as too tame for such a strong woman, but they were well suited to the character. Emma was never fully independent; even with her ability to hold her own in karate and judo, Steed was often her knight in shining armor, coming to her rescue at the end of each episode.

◆

Opposite: **Diana Rigg as Emma Peel in The Avengers**

Date: 1965

Silver grey/blue soft lamé jacket, bra and hipsters.

Right: **Two Designs for Cat suit**

Date: 1965

Figure 1: Black leather buckled to one side. Crepe roll neck shirt in white.

Figure 2: Black and white crepe.

1   2

Diane Rigg as Emma Peel in the Avengers.
White vinyl raincoat, with white hipster trousers
- part of the new wardrobe designed by John
Bates at Jean Veron. *London Life* Magazine.

Bates's designs brought a fresh look to the television series, particularly in his effective use of black and white contrast, which imparted an even more striking boldness to Emma's screen presence. Bates was dressing her in daring and youthful designs that were already part of his design oeuvre: see-through and bare midriffs; Op-art graphics, mini-skirts, and pantsuits. Emma's signature footwear throughout the series were flat boots made of sleek white leather with a bold black stripe down the center. The boots, like the clothes, were made for movement, and action, and, like Emma, captured the essence of what famed *Vogue* editor Diana Vreeland called the "Youthquake" of the 1960s.

The marked differences between Steed's and Emma's clothing is worth noting because the two characters were polar opposites in terms of sartorial style. While Emma's ensembles were the *ne plus ultra* in fashionable modern dress, Steed's were a deliberate throwback to Edwardian times, consisting of tailored suits with nipped waists, bowler hats, and an umbrella that served as a walking stick. The garments were chosen and designed by actor Patrick Macnee to present what he described as "a modern day Beau Brummell." While Steed's garments were made of standard suit fare such as wool, Emma's clothes often incorporated contemporary materials and fabrics such as ice blue lamé, white PVC, leather, stretch jersey, and vinyl. Steed's retro look even extended to his choice of automobile—he drove a vintage Bentley while Emma drove a streamlined Lotus Elan convertible.

The ultra-modernity of her clothing and character are ably captured in a newspaper article that ran in 1966, the year after Bates designed for *The Avengers*. "Actress Speaks Up for Pant Suits " ran the headline of a story that recounted Rigg being "turned away from a New York city night club and Montreal restaurant because she was wearing a white wool pantsuit." In real life, trousers were still not acceptable for evening wear for women. This story ran one year after the episode "Castle De'ath," in which Emma was outfitted in Bates's ice blue lamé hipster pant ensemble for a formal scene set in a Scottish Castle. A fictional heroine could readily wear such boldly modern clothes, but certain social contexts still restricted similar dress.

◆

There was a captive audience for the clothes, because of the runaway success of the series and the capsule clothing collection that was planned from the start of the collaboration with Bates. The copies of Emma's clothes were sold in department stores nationwide. The press coverage of the collection was impressive, filling almost a full scrapbook of newspaper clippings in the John Bates archive at the Museum of Fine Arts, Boston. The simple lines and graphic patterns of the original garments created for Emma lent themselves to ready-to-wear copies that were both attractive and affordable. Such was the success of the department store line that Bates had difficulty keeping up with the orders, and pirated copies abounded. The unlicensed copies were such a problem that Bates threatened to take legal action against the copyists with one journalist noting that they were "flooding" the market."

Even with such success, Bates stopped designing for the Avengers after twelve episodes because, according to his partner John Siggins, of the demands of producing his own collections and "attempted interference by producers in the design process" which is a frustrating position for any designer, especially for one whose bold and innovative fashions so effectively captured the dynamism, assertiveness, and vibrancy of Emma Peel and her "Emmapeelers."

John Bates: Original Drawings for **THE AVENGERS**

All drawings were done in 1965.

John Bates was well known for stylish ready-to-wear ladies clothing when he was quite suddenly asked to design a series of outfits for a TV show whose star was Diana Rigg.

The show was so popular that the producers decided to license John's designs to be sold as ready-to-wear. A selection of these designs follows.

Shiney white short P.V.C coat to be worn with skirts + trousers or on its own.

JOHN BATES.

DIANA RIGG
"THE AVENGERS."

White linen
trouser suit.
and
same in window
check (linen).

JOHN BATES.

Diana Rigg.
"The Avengers"

+ short skirt.

b/w gloves

Very Pale grey wool trouser suit with additional skirt.
White roll neck crepe shirt.

JOHN BATES.

Dana Rigg
"The Avengers"

Black + white
coat with
reversed
decoration of
faille ribbon.

JOHN BATES.

Diana
Rigg.

The Avengers

John Bates.

Diana Rigg
"The Avengers"

Mustard wool
suit. Trimmed
white plastic
and buckled.
White crepe
shirt

JOHN BATES.

Diana Rigg
"The Avengers"

Short grey
lizard jkt.
to mix &
match with
trousers &
skirts.

John Bates

Diana Rigg
"The Avengers"

Short B/W ②
coney coat.

to go
over
fighting suits
(black stretch
jersey).

JOHN BATES

DIANA RIGG

"THE AVENGERS"

SHORT B/W ①
CONEY COAT.

JOHN BATES.

Diana Rigg
"The Avengers"

White coat
+ trousers
outlined in
black faille
ribbon.

White roll
neck blouse.

JOHN BATES.

Diana Rigg
"The Avengers"

Grey "lizard"
coat short.
To be worn
with or without
trousers.

JOHN BATES.

DIANA RIGG.
"THE AVENGERS"

EVENING DRESS
WITH GUIPURE
LACE TOP &
STOLE.
THE GUIPURE
LACE SHOES.

JOHN BATES.

Diana Rigg
"The Avengers"
for dance of
the seven veils.
very minimal.

JOHN BATES.

SHARF FASHION HISTORY BOOK SERIES

**Larry Salk: California Dreaming
and the Evolution of American Fashion Art: 1945-1965**
Frederic A. Sharf with Susan Ward
Format: Softcover
Pages: 64
ISBN: 1-882266-18-8

Published in 2007 to accompany an exhibition entitled "American Fashion Art, 1945-1965" at the Sharf Admitting Center, Brigham & Women's Hospital, Boston, Massachusetts.

**American Fashion Art 1960-1990
Three Decades of Advertising Drawings**
Frederic A. Sharf with Susan Ward
Format: Softcover
Pages: 64
ISBN: 978-0-9818865-3-4

Published in 2008 to accompany an exhibition entitled "American Fashion Art, 1960-1990" at the Sharf Admitting Center, Brigham & Women's Hospital, Boston, Massachusetts.

**Style and the City: New York City Fashion Art
Two Decades of Advertising Drawings: 1955-1975**
Frederic A. Sharf with Morton Kaish and Alexandra B. Huff
Format: Softcover
Pages: 72
ISBN: 978-0-9818865-6-5

Published in 2010 to accompany an exhibition at Children's Hospital, Boston, Massachusetts.

**Exploring Fashion
The Art of Kenneth Paul Block 1960-1990**
Susan Mulcahy with Frederic A. Sharf
Format: Hardcover/Softcover
Pages: 64
ISBN: Hardcover: 978-0-9818865-7-2
Softcover: 978-0-9818865-8-9

Published in 2010 to accompany exhibitions at the Dana-Faber Cancer Institute and Sharf Admitting Center, Brigham & Women's Hospital, Boston, Massachusetts, featuring the art of Kenneth Paul Block.

**Fabric/Figure/Fantasy
Five decades of American fashion drawing (1940s-1980s)**
Alexandra B. Huff and Frederic A. Sharf
with Phil French and Morton Kaish
Format: Hardcover
Pages: 104
ISBN: 978-0-9839573-1-7

Publication produced in conjunction with the exhibition Figure/Fabric/Fantasy: Selections from the Jean S. and Frederic A. Sharf Collection of Fashion Drawing, February 25 – June 3, 2012, Loring Gallery, Museum of Fine Arts, Boston, MA.

**Beauty as Duty
Textiles on the Homefront of WWII Britain**
Alexandra B. Huff with Frederic A. Sharf
Format: Hardcover
Pages: 80
ISBN: 978-0-9839573-0-0

Published in 2012 to accompany an exhibition at the Museum of Fine Arts, Boston, Massachusetts.